What I Could Not Tell

by

Nettie Johnson

Acknowledgements

The story you are about to read is true. These are my experiences and how I remember them. The names of the people have been changed.

The events are from 1945 until the present. I am now 67 years old and a survivor of abuse. Growing up I lived without being able to tell. In the past abuse was not talked about. There were few professionals to help. Ministers, teachers and your own family would rather not acknowledge its existence.

I want to thank the many people in my life who have been there for me as support. God has always been there for me. My husband stood by me and loved me through all the ups and downs. My children did not always understand my tears but they loved me.

I would like to thank Paula Slemmer who, over the course of many afternoons, helped me write this story. I would also like to thank Carol Nase and Judy Yoder, who spent many hours, proofreading and typing, to make this book possible.

There were a number of people who encouraged me to write my story. One very important person was my father's cousin, Anne Heebner. She always told me she wrote her book about the history of a local township. Now it was my turn to write my book.

NETTIE FAMILY TREE

Granny b. 1887 d.1964 — m.1912 — Grandpop b. 1896 d. 1951

Grandmom b. 1887 d. 1944 — m. — Grandpop b. 1883 d. 1975

Wilson b. 1912 d. 1990 — m.1939 — Jean(Virginia) b.1919 d.2008 — dv.1949

Olivette(Snookie) b.1909 d.1983 — William b.1920 d.1999

James b.1954 d. — Matthew b. 1952 d.

John b.1948 d.

Thomas b. 1942 d.

Naomi b.1944 d.

Nettie b. 1945 d. — Adam b.1970 d. — m. 1970

Isaac b. 1946 d.

Hannah b. 1979 d.

Pepper B.1982 d.

Table of Contents

Part 2:

Chapter 1: My First Four Years

We all have secrets. They might just be an embarrassing moment that we do not wish to share. Or they may be secrets that gnaw at our souls.   Some secrets we try to forget and cannot, giving us a sense of shame or guilt and fear, especially if they would come to light. I have kept my secrets for many, many years. It was a learned behavior, a method of survival.

I was born in 1945. I have an older sister, Naomi, and two brothers, Thomas, the oldest, and Isaac, the youngest.

When I was born, the umbilical cord was wrapped around my neck and I turned blue. I had straight black hair and my mother would say I looked like what you would now call a Native American.

Some of what I write about my early years is what I remember and some is what I have been told.

The one story I am told about my early years is that I would throw up my milk. My father knew something was wrong and he was the one to take me to the doctors. I was allergic to cow's milk and was put on goat's milk. I also learned from my grandmother that I would cry a lot from pain in my abdomen. I had unusually messy diapers. My mother would leave me on the porch to cry. I continued to have the problem as I grew up. I have a spastic colon from bad nerves. Now I have medicine for the colon but have to watch what I eat. I also have occasional bleeding.

We lived in a small house for six people. I can only assume it was small as my crib was in the bathroom. I lived in this house until I was four years old and then my life fell apart.

I look at photos of my parents to help me remember them, especially my mother who had lovely dark brown hair and a "come-hither" smile. My parents made an attractive couple. My mother's name was Virginia and in slang terms was a "looker". She was called Jean by almost everyone. I am told she always enjoyed a good time. My father was a handsome man, but also the child of dysfunctional parents. He was most interested in having money. It was a mismatch made in Hell. My father worked as a car salesman and liked to pursue his "man's" life of hunting, fishing, sports and being a volunteer fireman. My mother was allegedly a "homemaker". She wanted a social life of dancing and partying. There were three children in diapers and no one to help her. My parents probably should never have married.

My mother never had the respect of her mother-in-law. No woman could ever be good enough for her only son. For example, it was not uncommon for Granny to rearrange all the furniture while Mother was away.

Anyone who knows our family would tell you I was one of four siblings. Yes, my father had four children, but my mother had seven, When the family separated my father took the four of us. We had a baby brother named John. John did not know his father. My father refused to acknowledge him as his son. My father told my mother that she could take John or none of the children. My mother took John with her. My parents went through a very bitter divorce. I was told that my mother was placed in jail for one night because she lied on the witness stand.

I was also told my mother had two boyfriends before the divorce. One was named Tom and the other was named Sam. She had a son named James and another son named Matthew. I was told that Sam had a heart attack and died. The other man is said to have committed suicide. That is all the information I have.

I have flashbacks of an incident: My father came home from work one afternoon and asked my mother a question. I was only a toddler and don't know what the question was. Whatever her answer, it angered my father and he called her a damn liar. He slapped her and she fell to the floor. My big brother, Thomas, herded us upstairs. I can see the incident like it was yesterday.

As a young child, I tried to tell my father about my time with my brother Isaac in foster care. He accused me of lying and of "making up stories". I am much older and wiser now and wonder if my father suspected our mistreatment and denying it to himself masked his guilt. But I am getting ahead of myself.

Chapter 2: The Horror of Foster Care

My mother took her son John and my father had the four of us. His mother was always called Granny. She was in her 60s. She told my father she was too old to raise toddlers. Thomas was seven and Naomi was five. They lived with Granny and my grandfather.

I was four and Isaac was three when we were placed in a foster home. I remember my father taking us into a large room with large chairs and a leather sofa. We sat there for a short time. After a while, my father stood up, went to the door, and turned to us. He said, "I will be back." He never returned. A strange woman entered and said we were to go with her. She drove us to a farm that became our foster home.

I am sure there are foster homes that nurture the children in their care. I am also sure there are some who take foster children for financial reasons. Because that money was so important we were given as little as possible. It was the "Perkins' order of the day", not to use all they received on us, their foster children.

Too much time has passed for me to remember how I felt. Maybe I did not think we would be there that long. We soon learned not to cry because we would be punished by having to eat hot peppers. I remember crying a lot because I wanted my mother and father.

Mrs. Perkins, one of the foster guardians, was a school superintendent. Mr. Perkins was a farmer. Much of the time he was not around. Many weekends they were away.

This left us at the mercy of their three teenage sons. I cannot remember their names nor can I see their faces. I just remember how big and strong they were. We had to listen to them and do what we were told.

The Perkins had rules for us that would be hard to believe. Isaac and I were not permitted to drink water from the well pump in the yard. We always had to ask permission for anything we wanted or needed. I can vividly remember a visit to the farm by my father and my older siblings, Thomas and Naomi. Naomi wanted a drink of water from the well pump. I cautioned her that we were not allowed. She insisted that I take a drink as well. I fearfully looked around and not seeing any of the Perkins family we took a drink. After my family left the Perkins confronted me about drinking from the well pump. My punishment was to eat red hot peppers. If you did not eat the first one you were given more just as hot as the first. To this day I cannot eat anything hot or spicy because it will burn my mouth.

Even these many years later I can picture the farm and all the buildings. It was a two story house with an attic. The bedrooms were on the second floor. Isaac and I slept in the same bed.   There was a big barnyard for the cows, pigs, and a horse. There was a field for the bull. The geese ran loose all the time and loved to chase us. And there was an outhouse, no bathroom. There was also a potato field. In the field I remember an airplane landing and catching on fire. We can still see the pilot and airplane. Fortunately, the pilot got out of the plane in time.

The Perkins' sons delighted in terrifying us. They had us convinced that if the stallion got out he would attack us, especially at night when there was only one light in the barnyard. Even if only one of us had to go to the outhouse we would go together. One of their tricks was to lock us in the silo and start filling it. We were locked in and could not reach the door. We did not know how to get out. We were trapped. The fumes from the silage were gassing us. We were screaming. Isaac and I were terrified. Someone came and got us out. Who? We cannot remember.

I also remember when the boys put us in a water barrel and told us there were snapping turtles at the bottom of the barrel. The boys made us believe the turtles would bite our feet off. We did not know how to swim. When the parents came home they got us out of the barrel.

The three of them became a mob, with a mob mentality. They would find all kinds of things to scare us. I can still hear their despicable laughter when they would kill an animal. They thought it was fun and laughed all the time.

Our early education was in a one-room schoolhouse with an outhouse for the boys and girls. I remember one incident so well. I was in the outhouse and got stung on my bottom. There was no first aid to help. I was made to stay at school until the end of the day.

School was better than being on the farm where the boys would shoot the pigs. It terrified us even though their father took care of the guns. I can still hear their despicable laughter. We were expected to help with the butchering that followed.

I would ask the Perkins for my mother. They lied and told me she was dead. Isaac and I knew what that meant because we saw all the animals die. My father would come once a month and take us to a place not far from the farm. It was always the same place because my father was only allowed to see us for a short time. I don't remember asking him about mother. I believed she was dead for many years.

Were we a symbol to the Perkins that they were poor and needed us for the money? We certainly were not a threat. But to the sons we were. They repeatedly emphasized to us we were not wanted there. We were not members of their family. Were they just greedy? I remember a total of five foster children living there for which they were compensated. Mrs. Perkins, who held a position of authority in the school district, had to maintain her image in the community.

I remember playing with Isaac in the haystack. The three brothers were there as well. How old I was I cannot remember but pain is difficult to forget. When I fell and broke my arm all that was done was to put my arm in a sling. Besides that, I do remember being sick a lot with childhood diseases and having high fevers. I had to stay home from school frequently. I had to stay in Mrs. Perkins office on the couch.

There was a girl named Sally that lived at a farm just down the road. She was my age and we were in the same grade in school. The farm belonged to her grandparents. I have warm feelings in my heart when I remember how we would play dolls together. Then one day she was gone. Sadness cannot describe how I felt. She was a respite for my life. My time with Sally was a time when I felt safe.

One day when we arrived home from school there was a terrible storm. No one was home at the time and we could not get in the house. We stood in the barnyard and got very scared because of the thunderstorm. All I could think of was to go to Sally's place to be safe. That night I was asked why we did not stay at the farm. I told them we were scared and could not get in the house. NO ONE WAS AT HOME!!! We were told to always stay there no matter what. Then Mr. Perkins beat me with a belt. I have scars on my back to this day from that beating.

One Saturday when the Perkins were away the boys tied my hands behind my back and a rope around my neck to hang me. While this was going on Isaac was running back and forth in front of the house screaming hysterically. The parents came up the driveway and saw what was happening and stopped it. Those boys did not get any punishment for any of their cruel deeds. I have nerve damage in my right wrist from the rope the boys tied around me. I still do not have total feeling in that wrist.

The Perkins were then given two small foster children. I can still see them in their high chairs. Again, I cannot remember their names but at the age of five I was to take care of them. One day one of the children took his diaper and put it in the hole in the outhouse. I had to get it out.

Isaac and I never had enough to eat. We were always hungry. If the babies did not finish their bottle or cereal Isaac and I would drink the milk and eat the rest of the cereal. I taught Isaac how to steal other food in the house when we were alone. We could always find potato chips, cake or water. The only food we received was what Mrs. Perkins put on our plates. We were always hungry. We were young, growing children.

One summer I remember very vividly when the Perkins went on a two week vacation. We were placed in the care of an elderly couple. It was like living with loving caring grandparents. They fed us until we were full. The lunches they gave us each day were glorious. It felt like we were in Heaven those two weeks. It was different than the Perkins' house. We got hugs and no punishments. We could not do anything that would require a reprimand.

Back at the farm another boy arrived. He became our only friend. His name was Joe and he lived in the attic. I would sneak up to his room to watch him paint pictures. It was a place of comfort. I do not remember how long he was there. But I missed him when he left. We laughed and I had a safe place for a short time.

Another memory I have is when Isaac and I would bathe in a wading pool in the back yard at night. Where did the Perkins family bathe? Again, my memories of this are lost. I do remember all the fun Isaac and I had together. We learned how to play and look after each other.

Besides taking care of two foster babies I had other household chores to do. I did dusting and cleaning, chores that I could do at my age. If the chores were not done to Mrs. Perkins satisfaction they were done all over again. Another chore Isaac and I did was picking up stones in the potato field. I remember many hot days out in the field. And of course we were not allowed to drink any water. Another job we did was carry two metal buckets of water to the goats in the field behind the barn. The goats would knock the buckets over and we would have to repeat that chore many times. To this day, I dislike goats.

When I was eight and Isaac was seven my grandfather, who had been ill for some years, died. The Perkins would not allow us to go to the funeral. Soon after, my father came to take us to Granny's house. It was 1953 and that is where the rest of the family lived. The Perkins would not allow us to leave with our BIG JAR of pennies, which we had saved for years. I was not allowed to take

Chapter 3: A New Beginning

I was eight years old and Isaac was seven when we joined my father and Granny at our home in the little village. Thomas was eleven and Naomi was nine. We had a difficult time adjusting to this new life. Those four years in foster care had changed us. The four of us slept in one room. Thomas and Isaac were in one bed and Naomi and I were in bunk beds.

Granny was good to us. She was like a mother. She must have realized by our ways and behavior that our life with the Perkins had been repressive. She had to remind us we did not have to ask if we wanted a drink of water. "Just get a drink," she would say. We were afraid to ask for seconds at dinner. We even got dessert. Granny was horrified when we chewed and swallowed chicken bones. But we ate them at the Perkins we told her. "Whatever you put on your plate you must eat," was Granny's mantra. But she did not mean chicken bones.

I can see her to this day. Her first name was Ella; Granny was tall, slim and wore glasses. Her white hair with yellow streaks was always pulled back in a bun. To keep it in place she used bobby pins and brown tortoise shell combs. She taught me how to do her hair, which I did when she was very ill. Her dresses, which she made herself, were long and colorful. Stockings were always worn and unattractive black tie shoes with block heels. We always knew by the sound of them that Granny was around.

One way Granny would punish me when I was bad or did not listen was to come up behind me and box my ears. She did this quite often. One doctor told me that was why I have a hearing loss. I also cannot hear sounds when the volume is high. I wear two hearing aids to this day. The rest of my siblings do not have to wear them. Granny had her own way of disciplining us.

She always took care of us at breakfast. Granny had breakfast ready for us in the morning. We could have cold cereal or hot oatmeal. These were followed by shoofly pie or funny cake, Pennsylvania Dutch treats, and a cup of Postum. We always had breakfast before we left for school. She would pack us a lunch of peanut butter sandwiches. In elementary school we would only buy milk for lunch.

If anyone asked us about our foster care, we were to respond with "Nosy People Don't Live Long." We did not know how to share what was ours and that was no one else's. Children change so much each year growing up. Those four years were a terrifying time. We had been away from our family for so long, you would have thought Isaac and I were adopted when we came home to the rest of our family. We had a very hard time enjoying a life of freedom and loving care. For the first time we could remember, Isaac and I were permitted to play in the yard outside. We were allowed to be children. They taught us street ball, baseball and football. A neighbor from across the street, Leroy, taught us basketball. We were overjoyed to become part of the neighborhood. Playing with other children also helped us understand the concept of sharing. We were used to being protective of what little we had in foster care.

School was also a big adjustment. We attended a big elementary school, so different from our one-room schoolhouse. It was our first experience with an inside bathroom. We had to learn to flush and wash our hands. We were overwhelmed by the amount of children at the school. The education we received at the one-room schoolhouse left us far behind the other students our ages. After I repeated third grade, Isaac and I were in the same class. We graduated together from high school in 1964.

There are some memories that I still have from over 50 years ago. It was a new life with Granny and Dad. We were poor but I remember having two dresses for school that Granny made for me.   And I had two pairs of shoes. Having two pairs of shoes was heaven. When we were in foster care, we had one pair for school, the rest of the time we were barefoot.

As every child will tell you, there are teachers you remember fondly and those you want to forget. Fourth grade brings back happy memories of my teacher, Mrs. Meek. I felt comfortable in her classroom; she never picked on me. She even made me Student of the Month. Fifth grade was a different story with Mrs. Curtis. My mind has not forgotten times that were embarrassing and hurtful. It is the rare person, and I have never met one, who could not remember an instance in their life when they wanted to disappear! I could not read the word "rapid". And she made me sit there until I could tell her. Why? I still ask myself. I felt humiliated. In sixth grade I had Miss

Cressman. She was stern but I had no problem with her. I learned a lot about art and enjoyed that subject.

When I was in that large elementary school I had a very hard adjustment and was often by myself on the playground where there was much equipment. Our recess time was very different at the one-room schoolhouse. There had been no playground equipment. All I can remember were some kick ball games and the girls played separately from the boys. My brother and I had limited social skills. We did not know how to share or play with other children.

My elementary school was a public school but religious education was available. If a parent sent in a permission slip, their child was allowed to go across the street from the school to a small chapel to receive instruction from two Mennonite ladies. We were allowed to go once a week for an hour. They had a big easel and used it to tell Bible stories. They were dedicated to their religion and the message I remember most was "God loves you." With the background in foster care, a mother I rarely saw and a father who never hugged me, I thought, "God doesn't love me." But the teaching of those ladies would stay with me in a positive way and would help me in the future.

We were poor; we had no indoor bathroom. Instead we had an outhouse. On Saturday night, a big metal tub was placed on the dining room table and Granny would bathe us. I remember in the summer Granny would wash Naomi's and my hair outside on the back steps. We would also get baths at the neighbor's house, the Jefferson's. They had a bathtub in the house and Mr. Jefferson would bathe me and Mrs. Jefferson would bathe Isaac. I did not question this unusual arrangement at the time. We had taken "baths" outside in the wading pool at the foster home. This was better. Did the Jefferson's teenage son notice me during bath time? I do not know. I was young at the time.

On Wednesdays Granny would go to her quilting time at her church. The Jefferson's son came into our house. He must have known I was alone. He demanded I go upstairs. I told him no repeatedly. "Do it!" he replied." or I will kill your Granny." I was gripped with paralyzing fear. Granny was the only real mother figure I ever had in my life. I did not know the word then but years later I knew the word, "rape". He would bite my breasts and tell me he wanted them bigger. He would take his hand all over my body. This went on until I was eleven years old when I got my period. He said he would not get me pregnant so he left me alone from then on.

When I got my period for the first time I was totally unaware what was happening to me. I was at a friend's house in the neighborhood and went home after I saw the blood on my underpants. I was sure I was dying. I had flashback of the boys shooting the pigs and all the blood and the laughing. My father and Granny must not have realized how frightened I was. I told them I was bleeding, something was wrong. Both of them, to my horror, laughed and sent me back to my friend's house. I was very hurt by their lack of concern for my feelings.

When people laugh at me I have a hard time. I think that is true of most people. My husband enjoyed laughing at me and making fun. Sometimes it would hurt my feelings. But he was not doing it to hurt me. I don't think my father and Granny knew how much they hurt me when they laughed at me. Also my older brother and my sister had no idea what laughing at me did. I would get laughed at in school. I had to learn not to take everything so seriously.

My neighbor became my teacher as she explained what was happening to me. She was only four years older than me but to this day she tells me that she was like a mother and a friend to me. That first period lasted two weeks. Granny sent me to a doctor who gave me a shot to stop the bleeding.

Getting my period at eleven created a lot of health problems along with all that took place with foster care. I did not communicate to my father and Granny the abuse, stress and anxiety that I experienced for four years in foster care. Then just when I felt safe, I lived in terror when the neighbor's son threatened to kill my grandmother. I Could Not Tell!

Our emotions contribute to the state of our health and my problems gave me a lot of pain. Granny always teased me that I could not handle pain and with that in mind would never have children. Before I would get my "monthly pain" I would have cramps and throw up. I would also have a migraine, which would usually require me to go home from school. Two times the migraines were so bad that I could not see. I was very scared and did not know what was happening. I was afraid to tell anyone except my

brother Isaac.

When I was around eleven or twelve years old, I

wanted to feel loved. My Dad reinforced his negative

feelings about me by telling me I was just like my mother

who he repeatedly called a whore. He said I was no good

and would never amount to anything. I wanted to get away

from the animosity and dysfunction of this house. I wanted

to move. Across the street was a wonderful woman, Mom

Largent. She had seven children with only two still at

home. She offered to give me a more stable, loving and

secure home. Mom Largent taught me many things. One

of my fondest memories was when she taught me to kill,

cut up, and cook or freeze chickens. We had many of

these great learning experiences together. She would

never argue with people. She was the epitome of a

pacifist. God was first in her life, followed by her family and her many friends. To me she was a very special friend and like a mother.

I remember a time when the three of us, Dad, Mom Largent and I, sat on the Largent's front porch. My Dad refused to even consider the possibility of my moving. What he said next was a complete surprise to me. "If anything happens to me," he said, "all four children will be sent to the Moose Orphanage in Elizabethtown, PA." That was about a hundred miles away. I was devastated by his solution and his lack of empathy: his total disregard of my feelings.

During my time in foster care I learned to steal as a survival behavior. At night when we were alone, I showed Isaac how to cut a cake so no one would know a slice was missing. I also taught him how to take just a few chips out of the potato chip bag.

In our neighborhood there was a corner store where all the kids went for treats, penny candy and ten cent ice cream cones. I wanted to feel like I was part of the group but I had no money. My father had a cup with his spare change at the top of the cellar steps in the pantry. It was so tempting. When no one was around I tried my hand at stealing again. I used the money for some treats with the rest of the kids. Somehow my father knew it was me. None of my siblings were seen buying treats like I was. No more money was ever in the pantry again.

There were times as I grew up and as an adult when I would have flashbacks about my stealing. I felt like Satan was tempting me when there were times I could have stolen again but did not.

I wanted a way to earn some money. I saw an ad in the newspaper for a babysitter. The ad turned out to be false. When I called the phone number, a deranged person was on the other end. I had to tell my father about the ad.

He went with me to meet the man. He never showed up.

What followed was a good job at a Jewish summer

camp. I was around thirteen years old. I would stay at the

camp from Monday until Friday. My duties were childcare,

helping with meals, and lifeguarding the children. It was an

enjoyable summer. My roommate was a girl who was a

little bit older than me. She made me realize that people

who are a different color from me are good people. That

was a very important lesson at that age in my life.

My Granny taught me how to shell peas, lima beans

and break string beans. She would can them herself. I

remember being the only child in the family to help. Our

house was located in a small village. It was at the six

roads. All the neighbors knew each other. Granny would

walk to a nearby farmhouse to buy eggs and I would

accompany her. She would always put on her good

bonnet. She taught me how to choose the best eggs and

how to pay for them. It was a short walk to another

neighbor's house to buy corn for fifty cents a dozen. They

knew we did not have a lot of money, so they would give us

a few extra ears. When I got a little older, Granny would let

me go alone. I felt good about Granny trusting me to make

good decisions shopping at the farms.

I wanted to gain the respect of the neighbors. At the

time I did not know what it was called but I had to become

a different person. I could not let them know who I really

was and what had happened to me in my younger years. I

learned to say what I thought they wanted to hear. I

thought if I did things for them they would care about me

and respect me. One way I could do this was to pick up

their mail. So I walked twice a day to the post office and

collected all the mail for the people that lived on my street.

There were more and more times at home when I

was unhappy. Times I wanted to just get away, to move to

a happier home, like the one across the street. It seemed

to me the world was happy but I was not. I was at a dangerous level of depression and decided to get away from being abused and not wanted. I went upstairs, out my grandmother's bedroom window, and onto the roof of the porch. I looked down and thought that if I missed the sidewalk and landed on the grass, I would not die. I would be in pain. I knew what pain was and did not want anymore. I looked to the sky, to God and remembered my Bible classes. If you kill yourself, you would go to Hell. So, I made a deal with God, "you stay with me and I will stay with you. I will live."

Chapter 4: My Teenage Years

I had lived with Granny, my father and siblings for four years now. It should have been a happy time but now I had many flashbacks and nightmares. They were triggered by my time in foster care and the sexual abuse from the neighbor. None of the people around me knew about the abuse. My anxiety from all of those events created in me a need to escape. Because of my nightmares I learned to "fly" in my dreams. I still remember vividly taking off and flying above the trees and up the road by my house. I found those dreams comforting. I could get away from everyone and everything that hurt. I would turn my head away and look; no one was behind me. I would smile because I felt safe. I WAS FREE!!

I soon entered my teenage years. The chronology

of these events is difficult for me to place. Because of our

high school renovation in 1959, our school was on a split

schedule, grades 10 to 12 went in the morning, grades 7 to

9 in the afternoon. Leroy, Isaac and I became the three

musketeers. We played many card games at Leroy's

house and the winter was a time for us to ice skate. All three of us have happy memories of that year.

Babysitting was a way for me to earn money and I also met some very good people. I became aware of how happy families like Floyd and Mary could be. At the same time I worked as a waitress at several establishments. One job included learning to cook. I felt serving people was only part of the job. The other part was feeling appreciated and liked by the customers. I made a dollar an hour. One week I worked 70 hours and made $70.00. That was more money than I ever imagined I could ever make.

In almost every town restaurant, there are some male regulars; you see them frequently. There was a UPS driver with whom I became friendly. I was flattered that he asked me out on a date. We had already had several dates when one Friday night, after babysitting, Jim picked me up. Driving home, he asked me to go away with him to the mountains for a weekend. I did not feel comfortable doing that. I spoke with Floyd and Mary about what he had asked me. They were very protective of me. Floyd had contacts in the community and the trucking business. He informed me that Jim was married and had a son. The next time I saw Jim I confronted him with what I knew. I never saw or heard from him again.

When I was sixteen, I wanted to quit school. I needed Dad's signature to do so but he would not sign. I don't regret that he demanded I finish high school.

I saved money from my jobs and at 17 I bought a car, a 1951 Chevy for $150.00. My dad was furious because I did this without his permission. He was also upset because I did not need his help or money. Dad always tried to control us by saying if we did not do things his way he would take us out of his will. Perhaps he felt threatened by my striving for independence.

When I was 18, Granny crushed her hand in the wringer of the washing machine. She would not go to the doctor to check if it was broken. Because of this the laundry became my responsibility. I had to learn to hang the clothes in the same order as Granny always did. This was done all year no matter the weather. I had to get up at 5:30 AM and do the laundry.

At nineteen, I graduated from high school and felt very good about myself. I missed many days of school my senior year because of plastic surgery on my nose. There were serious complications later. One night babysitting my nose started bleeding and Floyd took me home. Two days later my nose bled again. This time it would not stop. Blood was coming out of my eyes and ears. My brother and sister drove me to the hospital in my car. I got blood all over the floor and seat. Because of the excessive hemorrhaging I had to spend three weeks in the hospital.

After that incident I had my impacted wisdom teeth extracted. They were cut out of my jaw. This resulted in facial swelling and bleeding. I was unrecognizable. I was in the hospital for a week rather than the normal three days.

Soon after, Granny, who was now 77, became very ill. No one knew what was wrong with her. She had a lot of back pain and laid down more than usual. I do not remember her ever going to a doctor. One day she asked me to bathe her and wash her hair. I had never done this before. I discovered she had extremely advanced breast cancer. Granny had had cancer for four years and never told anyone, not even her sister to whom she was very close. It was a devastating shock to me when I bathed her and saw the big black hole on the side of her breast. I did not say anything to her but I told my father. My Dad called the doctor immediately. She was admitted to the hospital. She begged to come home. Granny died that week on a

Friday. Aunt Lizzie, her sister, was 88, 10 years older than Granny. She died three days before Granny's death. Granny passed away on the day of Aunt Lizzie's funeral on October 12, 1964, the year I graduated from high school. Neither knew of the other's passing. My father was to be a pallbearer for Aunt Lizzie. When we got the call that Granny had died, Dad left for Aunt Lizzie's funeral even after learning his own mother had just died.

I was very distraught and distressed. Dealing with the death of Granny, who was like a mother to me, was very overwhelming. I could not stay in the house by myself. I went to the neighbors for comfort. After talking to some of them I went to Mom Largent who comforted me.

I felt abandoned and overwhelmed. I was 19 years old. It was now my responsibility to take care of the house and yard. I did the food shopping, laundry and cooked for Dad and me. My only outside employment was babysitting.

My oldest brother Thomas was out of the Air Force and married. My younger brother, Isaac, was in the Navy having just graduated from high school. Naomi, my sister had been in the Navy for a year. I felt very much alone, especially without Granny.

After Granny's death and my high school graduation, I had to think about my future. I did not want to be a waitress or babysitter the rest of my life. I realized I had to investigate furthering my education. A local business school offered very good courses I thought I could take. I enrolled but before I even finished my first course I was offered a job as a teller at a small local savings and loan. I totally enjoyed that job and earned $50.00 a week.

Chapter 5: Getting a Job

Dad drummed into our heads that if you had a job to make sure you were always on time. We heard that over and over again. With my new job I had to buy new clothing appropriate for wearing in an office. I was still driving my 1951 Chevy. Somehow I had to save money for a new car while dressing nicely for my job.

I always liked working with numbers and office machines. Working at the savings and loan I learned to post transactions for savings accounts and mortgages. I learned to balance my cash drawer every day without a mistake. I became very good at that. I met some very nice people at this job and enjoyed working with my boss. Two of my co-workers I still see once in a while. There was one man who many had a hard time getting along with but I learned to deal with him.

I worked several years at the savings and loan. I felt I learned a lot and it was time for me to find a better paying job. I was hired at a bigger bank where there were a lot of women and only three men working. Of course, my boss was a man. In my first position there I learned how they did the teller drawer. I then moved on to work in the savings department. I also answered the phones, filed and met with customers. I enjoyed my job and the people with whom I worked.

I became good friends with three of the women. We would go out for lunch at a little restaurant next door to the bank. Over the years I have stayed in contact with them. One of the women, Chris, happened to live near the school I went to when I was in foster care. We did not make that connection until just before she died of cancer. I learned Chris was also a friend with Sally. I still have fond memories of Sally and me playing dolls together at her grandparent's farm when I was in foster care. I also did not

know that Chris finished high school with Sally. I was able
to spend time with Chris and reminisce with her before she
passed.

Chapter 6: Moving Out of the House

The house was almost empty; it was just Dad and I. For some reason we never got along. Whenever we spoke to each other we would end up arguing. After getting what I thought was a nice job, I started to go out more. I started dating Joshua who was older than me. I don't know if dad liked him. I never asked. One Sunday evening Joshua asked me out for dinner. Dad got mad because he wanted me to make his dinner. I told him I had a date and he would have to make his own dinner. He did not like that idea at all. At that point I thought to myself that dad was not going to rule my life. If I had a date I was going out.

On my 21st birthday in 1966, I had had enough. I was moving out on my own. My oldest bother helped me pack all that I owned and took me to a single room in a private house. It was a big room so part of it was a bedroom and part was a living room. The rent was an enormous sum of $7.00 a week. At the same time I decided to leave the church I attended as I was growing up.

I felt free; I was on my own. I did not have to report to

anyone. But, I was not totally free. I still had nightmares

that someone was after me. I would wake up crying and

needed someone to comfort me. I still had Floyd and Mary

in my life but I could not tell them anything. What would

they think of me? I loved their children and taking care of

them.

When they found out I was not attending church they

were not happy. They invited me to go with them to their

church, which was of the same denomination, Mennonite,

as I belonged to growing up. Today I still attend this

church. I met some really nice people over the years there.

A family I met had a sister, Marie, who was moving into the

area and she was looking for a roommate. She also had a

job at a local bank.

Marie was from a big family; She was one of

fourteen children. Even though we had different interests

we got along. We each had our own household chores. We took turns doing the cooking and shopping. We each paid our share of the rent every month. About a year after we moved in together we decided to move into a bigger apartment down the street. We each had our own bedroom then.

I was pleasantly surprised when she asked me to accompany her to visit her family in Kansas. I was nervous as this was my first airplane flight and Marie would remind me constantly that "you can't get sick". We had a very nice week with her family. Except for the night that there was a tornado watch. I was awake all night worrying about the storm while Marie slept soundly. We lived together for several years. We each married within six months of each other. We are still friends and enjoy each other's company. It was a number of years before I could tell her what happened to me growing up. She told me she thought something was wrong but did not know what it was.

Chapter 7: Out in the World

After working at the larger bank for two years, I received two weeks' vacation. I made plans to visit my sister in San Diego, CA for a week. For the other week I wanted to visit my dear friend Marci who lived in Phoenix, Arizona. We had a layover in Texas on the way to Phoenix. During the lay over a young man, Greg, got on the plane and sat next to me. We had a nice conversation during the flight and exchanged phone numbers. I gave him the number where I would be during my trip.

While at Marci's that Saturday night Greg called and we went out to dinner. We had a lovely time and I enjoyed Greg's company. I was flattered someone I had just met asked me out.

The rest of the week I spent with Marci and we had a wonderful time together. I met many of her friends and she took me to see where the business she owned was located. I met some of the people she worked with. Her house had a water-cooling system; I was cold for a couple of days. That did not last long because the temperature rose to 120 degrees later that week.

Marci took me to the desert; I was amazed at the plants that surrounded the area. We also went to a mine owned by her half-brother, Don. He gave me some small pieces of real gold. Another night we went up the mountain and could look down on the city. It was beautiful. All the lights in the city were so bright in the clear night. The last day of my visit, Marci and her husband took me to the airport. After boarding the plane I found a seat where I sat by myself. All of a sudden the lights in the plane went off. For a long period of time the lights kept going off and on. Finally the captain announced there was a mechanical problem. This made me very nervous. While in flight and in the darkness of the night I felt I would never see my sister.

When we landed in San Diego, I could not find Naomi. After all the passengers had left the terminal a man stood alone. He was an attractive man with white hair. He was looking for me. It was Naomi's husband, CP. He told me my sister was working. Naomi treated me to Disneyland, Sea World and we went shopping. We had a fun week together. I had a nonstop flight back home.

One Saturday after my trip I was visiting my brother, Thomas, and his wife when the phone rang. It was for me. Who knew I was there? It was Greg calling me from his Army base. He wanted to go to the movies that night. I remember I wore a dress to look very nice. After the movie we went parking. It was raining. We started to make out. He wanted more. He raped me and hurt me badly. I forced him off of me and demanded he take me home. I was bleeding profusely. I never told my roommate, Marie, why I was home early. The next day, a Sunday, the phone rang. It was Greg and he wanted to talk to me. I was so relieved Marie had answered the phone. He begged to talk

to me. I refused. Marie told him I did not want to speak

with him. He told her he was going to Vietnam. I really did

not care. I have no idea of his fate.

Chapter 8: Family Life

One Friday night the girls from the bank went bowling at the local bowling alley. There were two men bowling next to us. As they were getting ready to leave I pointed out to one of them that the red pin was still standing. I said to him, "You are not leaving with the red pin still in front are you? If you get a strike when the red pin is in front you receive a free game."

We started to talk, realizing we graduated from the same high school. We exchanged phone numbers and he asked if he could come and see me on Sunday night. He came over to my apartment two nights later. We talked for hours about school and the teachers we had, and what subjects we took. When he left, we walked down the steps; he said good night and Adam kissed me. We dated for six months and then got engaged. We enjoyed a lot of things together like a bus trip to Washington, DC to see the cherry blossoms. We also enjoyed frequent bowling at the place where we met. We decided there was no reason for us to wait to get married. Adam had a two-week reserve Army camp that summer and we missed each other very much. We were married six months later. We both wanted a wedding in the church we attended and the reception also in the church. We invited two hundred people. After the reception we left on a two-week honeymoon in Florida. We went up and down the coast of that state. We had a camper on the back of the truck. People could not believe we were camping on our honeymoon. We had a great time. I always dreamed of being the perfect wife and my friend Mary was a good example. I continued to try to make Adam happy by doing things for him. One thing I needed from him was to know that he loved me. He would always answer me by saying I should know that, he did not have to tell me. I was always afraid he would not come home or he would leave me sometime. At night I would wake up crying from flashbacks, but I could not tell him why. How could I tell him I was raped? When we were having relations sometimes I had to tell myself it was Adam loving me, no one else.

Before the girls were born, Adam and I had a good time travelling west and seeing the United States. To this day I do not think I was ready to have children. I had a lot from my past to deal with. But I still could not tell anyone. I was always afraid someone would come and take the girls if I told anyone. When Adam was at work, I was afraid something would happen to him. I would find myself calling him at work to see when he would be home. He found himself in trouble because I called him all the time. I had to stop that; it was putting a strain on our marriage.

When the girls were born I wanted to be a good mother. I wanted Hannah to always be neat and clean. If she got dirty I would change her clothing and wash her. I just wanted to take good care of her. My extended family would tell me to let her get dirty. I learned with Pepper, the second daughter, it was all right to get dirty.

Adam and I had more problems than we could handle. There were hospital bills for both of us. We both had car accidents that made money short at that time. Every time we got out of debt something would happen that put us right back into debt. I would work but did not make a lot of money. Adam would always say that it helped. If I was short of money I would buy less food at the store. I would always get a headache because of the memories I had as a child with lack of food. At that time we had a good-sized vegetable garden which provided a lot of the food we needed. The garden was a family affair. We all helped plant and pick.

At night the girls wanted me to read a story to them. I was uneasy doing this for fear I would not be able to pronounce a word. I was glad when they could read on their own. I loved to listen to them read. They each had their own books they would read over and over again.

I was not a very good cook. I hated following a
cookbook, and I had little teaching. Luckily Adam would
eat anything I made, with the exception of anything made
with cottage cheese. I had a problem with new recipes
because I did not know what some of the ingredients were.
If I made something Adam did not care for, he would say,
"You really do not have to make it again." He would never
hurt my feelings about the food.

Adam had a very stressful job driving an eighteen-
wheel truck for long hours. Needless to say, he was not
home very much, so I raised the girls myself. I had a lot of
emotional problems especially when he went on night work.
Some of my old fears came back. I was always afraid
someone would come and take the girls from me. When I
was home without Adam I was scared and frightful.
Watching television at night did not help my mind. I would
hear every little noise. One time we heard there was a

rapist in the neighborhood. In the bedroom I kept a baseball bat next to the bed.

When the girls were five and eight. I was unable to touch or hug them. My terrifying memories of foster care paralyzed me from being affectionate to them. I would sleep on the couch at night when Adam was at work. I would hear Adam's keys in the front door as soon as they hit the lock. I felt I could no longer live with the fears that I was having all times of the day and night. I was in my 50s and I needed help. My emotions were affecting my children and my marriage.

Part 2

Chapter 9: Intertwining Journey

Esther, my cousin, needed someone to thoroughly clean her kitchen. At that time I did not have a job, so I volunteered to clean it for her. My cousin and I had a very close relationship and I felt comfortable in her house. That was one day's work that became a new future for me.

I can't remember how it all began, but soon after, I was cleaning houses for a living. I never advertised but sometimes word of mouth is better. I knew the families I cleaned for and I felt safe going into their homes. I had very few fears and felt such a sense of accomplishment. This job energized me to clean my own house at the end of the day. I enjoyed this employment for ten years.

It was a perfect job for my family. I could work while the girls were at school. In the summer, they accompanied me and helped with small tasks. At some of the homes they could play in the back yard and I did not have to worry about them. Also some of the homes had animals they could play with.

Our oldest daughter Hannah, at this time expressed a desire to play the piano. Sam was recommended to me by a local music store as an instructor. At one of Hannah's lessons, Sam became ill. She seemed too sick to drive herself. I insisted on driving her home. To my surprise, the next day, there was a lovely bouquet of flowers at my door. They were from Sam. I called her and said that was not necessary. It made me feel good to help someone. I think it is true of so many of us. We feel helping others is so rewarding. It was the beginning of a long, sharing friendship. We have gone through many ups and downs together.

Soon after, we established a working arrangement, a bartering agreement. I would clean Sam's house and Hannah would receive piano lessons from her. Hannah continued playing piano for several years. Even after

Hannah stopped taking lessons, I continued to clean Sam's house.

I still remember a conversation Sam and I had many years ago about Hannah's ability to read. My reluctance to read with Hannah came from my insecurity and knowledge that I had limited reading skills. Sam felt confident I could improve. She gave me a list of library books to read. It helped me to be more relaxed looking for books in the library and I had some guidance from the librarian. After reading each book, Sam and I took time together to discuss what I had read and also to talk about how I felt about the book. She was very pleased with what I retained which was a sign of good comprehension. Sam continually encouraged me to read. Today reading is a favorite pastime of mine.

Another good memory from that time period was an aerobic class I attended three times a week. After getting to know and feel comfortable with Jody, my instructor, I felt

I could confide some of my story to her. She told me I needed more help than she could give me. She knew of a program at the local hospital concerning abuse. She encouraged me to attend. I asked Jody to go with me to the first meeting and she did.

I had not in any way anticipated how difficult that meeting would be for me. It was my first experience actually listening to others talk about abuse of different kinds and that it was not their fault. I sat there and listened to the leaders and felt like they knew my life. It was so hard to listen to them; I just could not take anymore. I had to leave the room; it was too painful.

I continued to have thoughts about what was said at the meeting. I could not concentrate at my aerobic classes. Jody suggested she take me to an "Abuse and Survival Agency". It was there I met Anne, one of the counselors at the agency.

She was a tall, beautiful woman with blond hair. How could she understand and deal with what I went through as a child? I was very hesitant to talk to her. She knew that in order for me to talk to her I would need to feel some connection to her. She told me about her double mastectomy. I realized she would understand what pain was as well as the invasion of one's body. It took a few sessions until I fully trusted her and she promised she would not take any notes during our appointments. I wanted to remain anonymous because of my fears of being discovered by anyone in my past. I made sure that my sessions were confidential. My husband worked, my daughters were in school, and none of them would know my secret, that I was seeing a counselor.

Anne could only see me once a week for a period of three months. Part of the program was to go to support group meetings. I refused to attend those groups. The thought of it made me very uneasy. Would I be able to listen to stories of abuse and then tell mine? Anne told me that if I went I did not have to talk until I was ready. While seeing Anne, I had many flashbacks and fears. Because I had been threatened as a child, I was also fearful of telling my past to Anne. I did not know that at this time everyone from my past was deceased.

I remember Anne getting upset if I cried. I did not realize it at the time that it was unprofessional behavior for her to react to my emotions during our sessions. I was not allowed to cry in foster care and when I was older and living with my family, it was still not acceptable. Isaac was the only one who showed compassion and understood my sadness, because we had grown so close during foster care together.

During a session, Anne said I would know when it was time to tell Adam about my life and when to attend group. I can't remember who took care of the girls when I decided to go to group. I think we had a babysitter. One

Sunday afternoon Adam and I went for a walk in a nearby park. It took time until I got up the nerve to tell him about my rapes. He was calm and listened to my story. I was much relieved to be able to tell him. He did not hate me, nor was he mad at me for not telling him sooner. He still loved me no matter what happened to me as a young person. It was time to tell him why I was seeing Anne.

Unlike my siblings I could confide in Anne. She was like the big sister I had always wanted. Anne was like my sister Naomi, a year older than me. We found that we were very comfortable with each other and could share things that we both liked. On one of our walks, we did role-playing. Anne was my mother and I played myself. It was a successful session. I expressed a lot of my suppressed childhood anger at my mother.

While going to group I became good friends with one of the women. One day I received a phone call from her. She wanted to know how I felt when my mother left me.

She knew from group that my mother had left me at a young age. I expressed my anger to her. Then she told me she wanted to commit suicide. I knew she had two small children. I was very emphatic that her children would hate her for the rest of their lives. To my knowledge that woman did not kill herself.

Anne told me she could only see me a couple more weeks. The first three months of counseling were held at the agency. I was at the end of my allotted time period. I was comfortable with Anne and did not want to discontinue our sessions. She suggested I find another counselor to continue the work we had started. Anne also suggested the group could get together. We did, for a late breakfast at a local restaurant. At that time Anne suggested we could establish a bartering relationship.

In exchange for an hour of counseling at her home I would clean her house the following week. I would receive payment of $20, which was the difference. While cleaning her house, Anne would call me to make sure all was going well. I had her permission to call her anytime I needed her.

We played tennis, took walks, shared meals and books. Several Saturday mornings we did aerobics together. On one of our walks I noticed a new aroma and asked if she was wearing a new perfume. Anne laughed and said no. I believed it to be alcohol. We shared personal experiences about our children and husbands. I later learned none of this should have happened. She was telling me her problems and needs. She should have been listening to me as my counselor. We became very good friends instead of having a professional relationship.

Anne wanted me to have more support from friends at church. My first resource was my church, but in the 1980s, abuse was never mentioned. A chance meeting with my minister led to some intense conversation. I told him of my living in constant fear. He asked how I could believe in God and live in constant fear. I told him a few things about my earlier years and the trauma that it caused

me. He did not understand and wanted to learn more

about abuse and how to help people. I was lucky enough

to have three women from my church that became my

mentors; they gave me wonderful emotional support. I

could call them any time of the day and evening, all through

the week. They understood and were very helpful. So was

my friend Sam, who after she knew some of my story, was

willing to listen to me and give me support.

Chapter 10: The Conferences and Heartbreak

I heard about a survival conference. Anne and I talked about it. By this time, Anne felt I was to the point of going to a "Survivor Conference", sponsored by the Mennonite church. Adam decided to take me for a dry run to the bed and breakfast where I would be staying during the conference. I was expecting a cordial greeting from the owner but was taken aback by the woman's outburst. She wanted to know why I was there and allowed to attend this conference at her church when none of her fellow parishioners could attend. By the time she found out about the conference it was full. My Mennonite Church the previous year, I told her, had presented it. I made my reservation six months earlier for survivors of abuse. She wanted to know what hymnal was being used because that would denote our Mennonite denomination.

The conference was held on a three-day weekend. It was open to all who were affected by or interested in abuse, caregivers, ministers, lay people and their families. There were many workshops to choose from; I could attend three.

On Friday evening there was a candlelight church service open to the public. The candlelight was beautiful to me but totally unsettling to other victims who had suffered abuse rituals. On Saturday evening at the church service there were no candles. A support group session followed each workshop. We were free to ask questions about the workshop we attended. We were allowed to tell why we were there. It was also a time for group sharing. While in my support group I met some wonderful people. I remember talking to the husband of a survivor. He asked me how to help his wife with the abuse she remembered. I told him just being there and not being judgmental was the most important thing. Just love her for who she is now. A woman named Carolyn facilitated the workshop. I remember that most vividly. She authored a book on abuse in the church. It is a subject that is rarely acknowledged by anyone. The most important part of the conference was my realizing and understanding how people have dealt with abuse in their lives.

In October of that year my family found out our father was having health problems and he was falling in the cottage where he lived. He lived at a local retirement community with his wife. She was in the hospital at the time with depression. After one of his falls, I had to take him to the hospital. They said he could not stay in the hospital and the home did not have a bed for him at that time. I was the only family member with a room for him on the first floor. I took Dad home for the night. The next day the home had a bed for him in skilled nursing. The family had until the end of the month to empty the cottage. It took the four of us every weekend to go through their belongings. It was very hard for us to do because we did not know what they would want to keep. As Dad became weaker we were told the cancer was spreading. We also learned Dad had sclerosis of the liver. During his illness I felt the need to stay with him more and more. One day when Dad had to go to the hospital he was looking at the calendar on the wall. We asked what he was looking for. He was counting the days until his birthday because he wanted to outlive his parents, which he did.

Thomas and I were with him during the doctor's visits. The nurses were a big help to us in understanding what was happening to Dad. When it came time to make decisions for Dad the four of us talked and decided together what was best for him. At that time I learned how to talk to the doctor, how to ask questions, and how to help Dad. I will never forget when I went to see Dad he would cry and I didn't know why. I asked the nurse why he was crying and she told me he only cried for me. During this time I found myself getting closer to my Dad and was able to forgive him for things in my past. These were things he did not acknowledge or understand I had gone through as a child. When I came to feed him one Saturday, he was not expecting me. He told me he loved me. That was a deep and lasting surprise to me. I had not remembered Dad ever saying that to me. I went every day for two months to feed my Dad lunch. We talked and watched television.

I learned many things from my Dad's death. I know how much he appreciated my visits every day. I learned how to visit the sick and those who were living in retirement communities. It is a good feeling for them to know people cared about them. It is also rewarding for me to see and visit them. It can make you feel better. Dad died six months later and I was very sad to lose him. I know he is at peace and not suffering from cancer anymore. At Dad's funeral I felt I could do the eulogy for him. My family was very surprised, pleased and happy that I did that for Dad.

Two years after Dad's death, I wanted to go to another conference on abuse. This time I was asked to be a speaker. I spoke to Anne about doing this. She said I was ready and wrote a letter to the committee letting them know I was her patient and it was fine for me to speak. I was asked to speak for about fifteen minutes but ended up speaking a half-hour.

The conference was for ministers and caregivers. As I walked up to the podium there was a rope lying next to it left on the floor by the moderator. It upset me and I asked him to remove it. I had a flashback to foster care. It was the type of rope the boys used to try to hang me. The man graciously apologized and removed the rope. As I explained to the audience they realized why I had such a negative reaction to that rope. But it would be many years later before I would be able to tell my whole story.

At this conference, I met a very nice man who was raped by his father. I also met several women who asked me why I wasn't angry and didn't hate God. I felt God had not raped me or abused me. Man did; God did not. My cousin, Esther, went with me to give me support. She knew some of my life story already. There was also a woman there from my church. She sat with us and to my surprise told me a counselor abused her. We became friends and talked many times for support.

After I spoke, a young lady spoke about being abused by a minister. She was trying for years to get him removed from the ministry and get him out of a leadership position. She had been unsuccessful for a long time. The conference continued with workshops to attend. I did not stay for them. My cousin had to leave to go to work. I also had had enough for the day.

After Dad's death I continued with my therapy with Anne. One day while cleaning Anne's house, as I had done for six years, I cleaned the dining room then went into the living room. There in the living room was a pile of new books. I assumed they were from the library, which Anne

frequented. The title of one book was <u>A Woman's Journal.</u>

I opened it and started reading about a giraffe and alcohol.

I realized it was Anne's handwriting. It was a very

disturbing passage to me. I was very concerned about her

reaction if she learned I suspected her of being an

alcoholic.

I left Anne a note. I lied that there was a problem at

home. I had to leave; I was very upset and thought this

would hurt our relationship. Anne called me that evening.

She wanted to know what was wrong at home. At that

point I told her I needed to see her. She demanded that I

tell her on the phone what was happening. She asked why

I had left her house and what was wrong. She would not

meet with me until I told her. I asked her if she realized

what she left in the living room. She did not answer. I told

her that I found a book in the living room and after reading

one page I knew it was her handwriting. She became

furious and was yelling at me. I quietly told her this conversation had to end and hung up the phone.

I took my children to my sister-in-law's for the night. I did not explain any of what had occurred. My emotions were in turmoil. I kept saying to myself I killed Anne; I had killed my relationship with her. I just wanted to go to sleep. I opened a bottle of Tylenol, dumped some in my hand and swallowed them.

I realized I needed help so I called my friend, Sam. She called Crisis Hotline. When Sam arrived at my house she told me whom she had called because she did not know what she would find when she got to my house. I continued to say I killed Anne and just wanted to go to sleep. Adam did not come home until late so he did not know what happened. Saturday Sam took me to a clinic. I talked to a counselor there and said I did not want to stay. The clinic called a counselor in the area. Her name was Dr. Jane Greenburg. She spoke to me at length. I promised I would see her on Monday. After three sessions

with Jane I could not promise I would not hurt myself. She

convinced me I needed more help than she could give.

She suggested I go back to the clinic and be admitted.

One day at the clinic, I took off on my own. I walked

into a surrounding field. I just wanted to get away from all

the hurt. A counselor found me and gently explained the

procedures to me. I had a group session every day and for

an hour I also had an individual one with a psychiatrist. I

still did not want to reveal who Anne was. I did not want to

get her in trouble. Besides the sessions, I had time to write

about how I was feeling and think about my relationship

with Anne. I shared my room with a nice young girl. We

spent a lot of time talking which passed the time. It was an

experience I have not forgotten.

The doctor who worked in the young adult unit of the

clinic came to see me. He was asked by Jane to talk to

me. His goal was to make me realize I had done nothing

wrong. Thankfully, he was successful. He helped me realize Anne was supposed to be the professional and I was the patient. While at the clinic one of the doctors had a chance to talk to my husband. He explained to Adam how hard the situation was for me to let go of Anne and that it would take a long time for me to put the situation behind me. After my release, I continued therapy with Jane.

I have been a patient of Jane's for sixteen years. I remember when Sam showed me an article in the newspaper about a woman who had been in therapy for seven years. I said "No way. I won't be in therapy that long."

In the beginning, Jane and the doctor from the clinic worked together. They felt strongly that a letter from them should be sent to Anne. This was an imperative action to help with my recovery. Jane only wanted three sessions with Anne, her and me. The first session, Anne took no responsibility for any part of the situation, and what happened to me. After the phone call from Anne that first night she said she had no idea what to do or what happened to me. At that point I told Anne in a forceful voice that she could have killed me. After the first session we left at the same time. In the parking lot Anne wanted to hug me. I backed away. No words were spoken. Jane recommended Anne see a counselor. The counselor was president of the counselor's association and well respected. Anne went but was not pleased about going. She did not appreciate being told how to counsel other patients.

In the second session, Anne was most concerned about her financial situation. She wanted to buy a new car and was concerned that her funds would be tied up in a lawsuit. Anne contended that what I read was only her dream. I did not leave that session the same time as Anne. I stayed to talk to Jane. I was furious that Anne had shown no concern for me and how I had suffered. Jane and I decided three sessions would be of no help to me. She also recommended I retain a lawyer. I decided to go to a local lawyer and was emotionally drained after explaining what transpired between Anne and me. It affected me so much that I had to seek medical care on my way home. My lawyer contacted the agency and found out Anne was not a licensed counselor. A license could not be taken away from her.

My goal was to end our friendship in a friendly manner, but it was not to be. Within a year, a settlement was made out of court. I received compensation and never saw or spoke to Anne again. I received a letter from Anne's lawyer stating I was not to contact Anne.

Even though the legal issues were settled, that did not mean they were settled emotionally for me. Jane and I had to work through all my issues that developed because of Anne's unprofessional behavior. It took me time to understand Jane was not my friend. I had to start at the beginning with Jane, back to the days of early childhood and foster care. But most important was the procedures of proper counseling. We talked a lot about what Anne had done wrong. Jane constantly reminded me I was the patient, not Anne. My time with Anne did not yield healthy outcomes for me because it was unethical treatment. I learned my emotions did not affect Jane and I could cry and say what I needed to say.

A few weeks later I communicated with the Abuse and Survival Agency and was told Anne no longer worked there. I asked if it was connected to my situation. They replied there had been several other incidents with patients, which was cause for her dismissal. The agency told me I was entitled to the records of my sessions with Anne. When I received them I was floored at all the mistakes in her notes; the notes she said she did not record.

I still had a lot of therapy to do with Jane. I had so much to learn about what had happened to me as a child. I had to realize it was not my fault. I had nothing to fear. I should not be ashamed or feel guilty. When I told Jane my story, I realized I would not get hurt or killed. No one would get hurt, not my husband or my children. I became free to reveal what I could not tell.

Chapter 11: Memories of My Father

My father died May 4, 1990; I was 45 and no longer had to prove anything to anyone. All my life I had to show that what he said about me was not true. Granny always said I could not have children because I could not withstand the pain. I would amount to somebody. I would not be like my mother; I could stay with one man. Granny and Dad were wrong about me. I had goals for my life. I wanted to be a secretary and work in an office. I wanted to work with money because I enjoyed math. I wanted to be a good wife and mother; I loved children. These were my ambitions in life. I knew that God was with me and that he would help me all the way. These are the things I hoped for and wanted for my life. I knew I would not have a lot of possessions or money in my life. Whatever I could accomplish would be enough.

After Dad's death I decided to try my hand at college. I went for several years, taking one or two classes at a time. I was still working so I went in the afternoon.

The girls were in school when I went to school and at night

we had fun sitting around the table doing homework

together. Sadly I was not able to get a degree in General

Studies. But I did enjoy that education and learned a lot

from what I did complete. I especially enjoyed the English

courses.

Life was not all bad as a teenager. I have some

fond memories. I can think of the times Dad would take a

week of vacation. He would take the four of us to the

mountains. We could go swimming, fishing, or just take a

ride in the boat. We were all old enough to be on our own

and do whatever we wanted. Dad and I would do a lot of

fishing in the early morning. He would wake me up at 5:30

AM, get the gear together and off we went, just the two of

us. We would usually fish until 9:30 AM or so. One day I

caught the biggest fish of the day. We would usually go out

again after supper until dark. I slept very well those nights.

In the afternoon we would swim at the docks after all the boats went out. We stayed at a cabin that was owned by two of Dad's friends.

Another time we all went to Canada for two weeks. Again we stayed in a cabin that was big enough for the five of us. Dad also invited Richard along, whom we all knew very well. The first day we were there we went water skiing. When it was my turn to ski I fell. I went under the water and one of the skis hit my leg. Thank goodness I had a life jacket on. When I came up out of the water I had pain in my back. I turned over face up and floated until my brother got to me with the boat. There happened to be a nurse nearby so I did not have to go to the hospital. She looked at my bleeding leg and told me to stay off it for the rest of the time we were in Canada and see a doctor when I got home. When I got to a doctor, she said I had crushed a vein in my leg. If I did not get a shot every day for a week in my leg I would develop blood poison.

I also will never forget the time just Dad and I went fishing without the boat. We went up towards the mountains. We fished off the land and had a good time. I don't remember if we caught any fish. On the way home I was driving and all of a sudden there was a black bear in the middle of the road. Dad was sleeping, of course. I yelled! Dad woke up right away. I asked him what I should do. He said just keep driving; he will move. It turned out to be a baby bear and he ran. Dad and I had some good times fishing but when you fish you do not talk, so I never told my Dad about my life.

Looking back now I realize how much our relationship changed over those many years. During my years growing up, Dad was not there for me in a caring or supportive way as I tried to transition and adjust from foster care. My teenage years found a separation between us. I learned to be independent and accomplish things on my own. I learned to make my own decisions, which my father did not appreciate. When I moved out of the house I was on my own and we had no contact with each other.

Four years later I told my father I was getting married. I asked him to walk me down the aisle. It was a joyous affair and our relationship was renewed and grew in a positive way. He heartily approved of my husband and adored his two granddaughters. He loved to tease them.

Almost without me realizing it the feelings I had towards my father softened. We had a relaxed relationship. We did not argue; we had a loving time together. Who would have known many years ago I would have a hard time letting him go?

Chapter 12: Meeting Mother

My mother's only sister, Aunt Snookie died in 1983.
Thomas, Isaac, Naomi and I went to the funeral together,
our father did not attend. We were at the cemetery when
two people approached us from the road. We did not know
who they were. Our cousin told us they were our uncle and
mother. Mother didn't know us. Mother thought my brother
was my cousin.

We learned soon after the funeral that the two boys
in the back seat of her car when she visited us at Granny's
were our half brothers. She never told us who their father
was or why they had the same last name as us. Thomas
asked her if he could go hunting on her property and that is
when he met Matthew, one of those half brothers.

That night, after the funeral, I called my uncle and
talked to him for hours. I asked him if he thought Mother
would want to see us. He gave me her address and phone
number. I wrote her a letter in which I asked if she wanted

to communicate with us. We did not want anything from her. The four of us just wanted to see her again. After my letters, Mother and John, her husband, agreed to meet with the four of us at my house. We visited and talked for a long time.

Mother told me Dad had put a restraining order on her and she was not allowed to visit Isaac and me in foster care. I had never heard that. When I was young and living at Granny's, Mother would have to call first to get permission to come and visit us. We never knew if she would show up or not. When I was 12 years old I was in the hospital with appendicitis. My mother called and asked to talk to me. She said she was coming to see me but never did.

As years went by I hated my mother more and more. It was a long time until I even knew her name. I learned that she was married and seemed happy for once in her life. She had not told John, her husband, she had four other children. When I had the girls I could not understand her at all. How could she not care about the four of us, her children?

After Mother and I had spent time together, I had to realize she was no longer my mother. God had given me the time to spend with her and release the hate I had for her. I had to understand she was just another person. I could live at peace not having feelings for her.

Mother always said when she went to church she sat in the front pew because she belonged there. Years later John died. Mother had to move into a retirement home. She lived there until she was 86. I was not able to visit her because she lived far away and I did not know how to get there by myself. Instead of visiting in person, I would call her every week. I continued to call until one day she did not know who I was. She died soon after that. I did not hate her anymore. I just did not have a loving mother. I have no idea where she is buried, but to me that does not

matter.

Chapter 13: The Seven of Us

In 1992, there was a 50th birthday party for Thomas. It was the first time I met Matthew, my half brother, and his son. The next time I saw him was at Mother's house. He is a very quiet person and his wife is the opposite. We talk on the phone a lot now. He happens to live close by.

Another time I was at mother's house I saw a picture of James, our other half brother. I asked Mother how she got the picture of Thomas. She told me it was not Thomas, but James. To my surprise they looked very much alike. I had never met James before. When I talk to James on the phone I can't tell which brother I am talking to, they sound so much alike.

Thomas, Naomi and I decided to have a picnic with just the seven of the brothers and sisters. Everyone attended except James, who lived in Iowa. We also learned that John and James don't get along well.

Several weeks later, James and his family came to visit. They stayed with Matthew. I recall the first time I met James. He looked and talked just like Thomas. When I hugged him he was like a big teddy bear. I fell in love with him and his family right away. Adam and I went to visit him in Iowa in 2011. I enjoy seeing him. He is very outgoing.

After many years I finally met John. Naomi had been in touch with him. We decided to go visit him at his home in another state. We had a very enjoyable time and have been back several times. The seven of us shared many stories after discovering each other. We learned all of us had been through tough times growing up. Our half brothers had lived in 18 different places. We discovered that in many cases they had lived close by. We all have grown and we are all good people. It comforted my siblings and me to know we are all stronger for our hard times as children. I think Mother was relieved to know all her children finally knew each other. She no longer had to hide

us from each other.

Chapter 14: The Wall We Build

As we live with abuse, physically and emotionally, we develop a wall around us. The wall becomes a defense so this abuse does not happen to us again. We don't always know it is there but at these times it comes up to protect us from harm.

That wall goes up when anyone, someone we know or do not know, is a physical or mental threat to us.   The wall comes up to somehow stop the abuse. We are not always aware of the wall until afterwards. This wall prepares us for what we have to do to protect ourselves. When we are out for a walk our ears are tuned into the surrounding noises. At the store or a mall we watch people and what they are doing. I am always on the alert for a sudden noise or movement.

Mental abuse is as damaging as physical abuse, they both hurt deeply. If you are with a group of people who are saying things that make you uncomfortable that wall goes up. Those people can be family or friends. Both can hurt your feelings. You believe in God and another family member does not. They are tearing God apart in front of you. It hurts you badly. I would excuse myself and leave because I did not need to hear that. I live in the country, so when I go for a walk I have to be very alert to my surroundings and listen for all kinds of noises. When I am in the city I never walk by myself. At night it is harder to be alert and have the wall up all the time. When the girls were young I would always take them with me wherever I went. I would never leave them in the car for someone to take. I wanted to know they were safe.

I learned about the wall during therapy sessions. If the counselor was talking about something that I did not like to hear, a wall would go up to protect me from the hurt and I would be silent. It took me time to build trust with a counselor and feel safe with her. She was there to help me understand that what happened to me was not my fault. It took me time to get over the guilt I felt. I always thought I

did something wrong and would have to live with the

shame of it. I lived with fear of hurt and loss for a long

time. Jane helped me understand all this and my life is

now different.

Chapter 15: How Well Do We Wait?

When we are little children we wait until we can walk and talk. We wait until we are old enough to go to school. We wait until we can drive. We can't wait until college or until we are old enough to leave home. Society can't wait until we are married. We wait nine months for each child to be born. Life goes on and we wait until the children are out of the house. If we are lucky enough, we wait for grandchildren. Then we wait until it is our time to go see God in Heaven. Life is full of things for which we wait. God gives us the strength and time to wait. Everything is in His time. During life's waiting we have our ups and downs. We have the good and not so good times in life.

These are the learning times of life. They are lessons we learn and experiences that will help us to help others. During these times God is caring and carrying us. They are scary times and hard times. Times when we are afraid we won't make it through. But with our faith and love of God with us we will survive. We become stronger and

by faith, our faith grows.

Chapter 16: Personal Thoughts

Everyone has a cross to bear, and we never know what it is going to be. Why do bad things happen to us? Why are some people's burdens worse than others? I feel I have had an extremely difficult cross to carry for a very long time. I did not know how I was going to live my life with the fear. I could no longer live with the fear and pain because it was so debilitating. I realized I had to have someone to talk to. I had to find a person whom I could trust and with whom I would feel safe.

I, through learning how to deal with the fear, guilt and shame, live a different life. It is not my fault and I did not ask for it to happen to me. I have the desire to help other people. I don't want others to have to live like I did. I know there is help and relief for these bad feelings. That is why I wanted to write this book. If I can help one person live a happy life, it is worth telling my story. While I was writing this book, which was not easy to do, I had to keep in mind what my purpose was in writing it. The hard part was in remembering the old hurts, punishments, and remembering how people would put me down. To think about how I could get hurt if I told my story. To learn that a person who I trusted was treating me in a very unprofessional manner was hard to accept. Learning who the boys were in the back seat of the car and why Mother was hiding them.

My family does not feel the same about telling my story as I do. They do not want me to bring up the past. They think it will just hurt people and do me no good. They cannot see how it will help anyone. My oldest brother said, "There are so many books out there on the subject of abuse for people to read." I know my siblings have experienced different things - same time, same place, and different feelings.

I know they wondered why I had to write my story. I hope I can help them understand why I feel the need in my heart to help other people.

In my life I was lucky to have had the chance to go to Bible School and learn about God. I feel He is a big part of my life and helps me make decisions that are right for me. I need Him every day to help me make choices and help others in pain. With his love and guidance I can somehow cheer up people who are sick or living in a home. This is my mission, to help others.

I pray I have years to live so I can continue to enjoy the sun, birds singing, quiet times and relaxing. There are many things in life I have learned to appreciate and enjoy. My family is very important to me. I continue to need all the friends I have. I love making new friends.

The best part of the story was the relief I felt after releasing all the hate and anger that had built up inside me all those years. I no longer have the fear I did growing up.

I can live in peace knowing I did nothing wrong. I can love

my family and they can love me for who I am now.